SO MANY THOUGHTS START WITH THE LETTER I

Sarah Pledger

*This book could not have existed without all that has made a home
inside my house, welcomed or not.*

*To the ones I love, who helped me open the door. This is, in part, for
you.*

*The rest, I dedicate to the little girl who used to carry
around a sparkly notebook for her stories and tell everyone
she was going to write a book. Sorry I took so long.*

CONTENTS

INTRODUCTION

I have always found that there is a power in words.

They have a universality to them that allows them to, perhaps contradictorily, be incredibly intimate. One person, in writing of their own experiences, can inspire another to relive their own. Cause them to grip the page a little tighter, take a breath that's a touch heavier and think, *this is me*. In that moment, there is two people who have been personally affected by those words, and in that same moment shared that feeling across a space connected by the simple bind of ink. That is a powerful thing.

I have always wanted to write a book. That, in itself, is not a unique dream. Nor is the final product, with its standard formulation of pages, bound together in a way that is fairly typical for a collection of poetry, hardly far removed from the norm. That's okay. More often than not it is the journey, not the destination wherein the transformative lies. The wonderful [and daunting] in-between where words are picked like flowers, and arranged by hand to form a new bouquet.

Every word written in this book has been spoken, written, sung, and thought a thousand times before. Yet, I have chosen to write them again, to my own beat. For I believe we can re-read these words, in as many thousands of ways as they can be re-written, and still find new ways to connect to them. I can only hope to re-arrange the words that are available to me, to reach new meanings that are universally felt, and intimately our own.

Poetry was not my first love, but it has become my greatest refuge as of late. It has been there in times when finding the right set of words, in the correct order, and with the proper syntax to covey the true depths of my emotions has felt near impossible. Though this anthology is not necessarily always about me [despite how many times I use the first person], it is an extension of me and, beyond that, in our infinite connection over the millions of words available to us, it becomes something to be shared.

Even if just one short line of a poem in this collection has you pause, for a moment, catching you in a flash of recognition, then I shall be glad. If only to offer you that sensation of being seen which reminds us all that nothing is truly felt alone. A feeling that the words of others have so often captured in me.

So Many Thoughts Start With The Letter I

Which of these words have you heard before?
Probably, most likely, almost certainly, all of them.
I suppose I can only hope I have placed them in an order
that can hold some meaning to you.

UNBROKEN

you are the most fragile.

ART

is a mirror

someone may have made the mould
poured life into it
sweated and bled and cried over it
polished it to shine

but we all see something different
when we look
because when we look

we look through a kaleidoscope of lives

FRACTURED

Every time I speak
I give away a piece of me,
a part of the puzzle,
a fragment of a larger picture,
splintered unconsciously
or gifted
        generously.

Regardless of my intent
when I hand you a new piece,
it is yours to keep
or discard as you please.

WELL-FORMED

A good poem is well-formed.
The structure is well-fitted.
Rhyme and rhythm are metered,
steady and true and—

well,

it seems to me,
that that's far too neat
all too clean
for someone like me

and what are rules
after all,
if not meant to be bent
a little out of shape,
if not

broken

when the subject matter itself is not made
to be curved into a perfect circle.

BLUFFING

How do you show the world
that you smile when you're happy
and you cry when you're sad
when emotions stand so far away,
behind triple-glazed glass
and barbed wire fencing
and a mirror image that stares back,
empty.

Is it a good poker face,
or are the cards in your hand all blank.

DEMONS

I've realized I can't hope to claw my way out of the
shadows
without confronting the demons that dragged me there
first.

Shall I meet them in a battle of wits, of wills,
show them a mirror and see who cracks first.

Prise open my head and let the light shine in,
force them to claw out their eyes to stop the burning.

Offer them a rose, soaked in poison,
and watch the thorns do their work.

Take the scattered remains of dreams long destroyed
use them as kindling, to start a fire and reduce them to ash.

Lead them deeper, far deeper into the depths,
till the pressure rises and they're choking on their breath.

Or shall I fight with the daggers
I must pull from my own chest,
left lodged there in the hopes
that it would stem the blood
from flowing freely
from my damaged heart.

I suppose it doesn't matter
whichever route I take out of the dark,
I'll leave the same bloody trail upon the path.

CONSCIOUS THOUGHTS

I have expectations piling on top of
dreams left scattered like broken shards amongst
hopes that fall short in the face of
reality which cracks in spidery lines across my
imagination, a flickering flame on a candle
close to the end of its wick.

A PANIC ATTACK

my heart's pounding
I can't breath

you'd never know

my mind's racing
I'm losing time

you'd never know

your lips are moving
I can't hear the words

you'd never know

I nod
I smile
I laugh

you can't know

I'm scared
I'm freaking out
I want to cry

I can't let you know

I'm tired
exhausted
of running in circles

so that you do not know

I say goodbye
though
I want to speak

but I won't let you know

why?

my heart's pounding
my skin's freezing
I'm sweating
I'm dying

I can't breath

I'm scared
I'm tired
my mind's lost
in what ifs
why did you do thats
stupid
stupid
stupid

but you'd never know

you wave goodbye
I smile
it doesn't shake
not like my hands

you'd never know
you can't know
I won't let you know
why?

I—

I do not know.

FEAR

I'm not scared of my thoughts—
I fear what they know about me.

MY DRINKING SONG

I'm funnier, drunk.
I'm more bold, off my face.
I have so many stories to tell,
       to make you laugh
     to make you like me.
        They all start
           'I was drinking.'

                  Hm.

    Is that who I am?
    Is that all I am?
    I don't have the courage
    to find out
    without shouting

       'One more'
       'One more'
       'One more'

See,
thing is—
here's the thing

Sober,
I'm not always right.

         Inhibitions are such a downer.

But...   with a drink in my hand,
      several empty glasses by my side,
      my mistakes are genius,
      brilliant gems of stunning stupidity
      for you to cut your teeth on   ...oh.

I've embarrassed myself,
made a mess of myself,
done a number on myself,
as many times
as I've made the night
            Is that what I want?

                        Hm.

I think I'll have one more,
if you please
just to—
just to tide me over
            honest.

                Truth is, there's never just one
                    because one isn't enough
                        make me funny
                            brave
                stupid enough to make mistakes
                that end up humorous footnotes
                    in someone else's story.

    Isn't this grand?

            The best me I can be
            drunk! at my worst

RESTLESS MIND

I can't sit still through movies
I struggle to finish a story in multiple parts
Don't ask me to find the end of this sentence
It's already been lost down the back of the—

Half-finished projects litter my bedroom
Half dreamed ideas litter my head
Don't ask me what I'm going to do next
I've already left it abandoned
in the bottom of the drawer.

I talk too fast, I know
In ink, I get desperate
Miscount letters
Misspell words
In a haste
Always a rush
Fill pages
Disjointed
Capture this feeling

Before I find a new thread to unravel
So many threads, tangled
My focus is gone
So often moving away
Come back
Come back
Come ba—

It's hard
and too easy
to sleepwalk when you're wide awake.
That project?
I can't see it, it's not there.
That promise?
Left on unread.

What do you want me to do?
Does it even matter?
My mind has already moved on.

How
I ask
do I try

to write everything down that I feel
when it requires the patience
to sit still and the time
to fill a book and the ability to tell you
what's on my mind when the truth is
in all honesty it is just as relentlessly
ridiculously repentantly
restless

as I—

SONG LYRICS

I wrote song lyrics on my skin,
made it permanent.

Imagined the ink would sink through the layers,
slide into sluggish veins,
sing me a melody,
one that I could follow.

EXCUSES

They have a lot to say,
we've heard them all before.

They're a liar's refuge,
a poor man's currency,
deflect from the problem,
reject the solution,
hide from your mistakes.
Where does that get you?

Excuses, excuses.
They so often find a way,
to justify,
to redirect,
to obfuscate,
procrastinate for
procrastination's sake.
Where will that land you?

Excuses,
what a joke,
your sheep's coat
is wearing thin,
thin as the lies you spin.

Excuses,
what a laugh,
I fail to see what you gain
by playing me for the fool,
am I a joke to you?

Excuses,
what a shame,
you know you won't be taken seriously

until you stop spewing these preposterous—

TRYING

I'm trying.

I think.

Sometimes,
not all the time,
I'm trying.

It's too quiet,
sometimes.

Nothing here to remind me
that I have a voice
or a smile
or a personality.

It can get too loud,
sometimes.

My mistakes speak clearly,
my flaws stand on display,
my future comes after the beep.

It is busy,
on occasion
with occasions.

I paint on a smile
and I laugh from a can.
It's the closest I can get
to screaming.

At those times
I don't know if I'm trying,
or steadily losing my mind.

Other times,
I want to try.
I really do.

I have dreams and hopes,
crazy ideas and
realistic expectations.
A plan.

But I'm not trying,
I'm not doing much of anything.

It's too loud.
It's too quiet.
There's static
and cotton candy.
It doesn't exist.

I don't exist.

Why does trying
try so hard
on those of us
who do their best,
be patient,
put one foot forward,
give it their all
when that all
is the bare minimum
to everyone else.
Oh, isn't it all very trying.

This is me,
trying.

But I'm a bad multi-tasker
and there's so much to do.

Moving is work.
Thinking is work.
Breathing is work.

I can't work on everything at once
and I have nothing left to give

except,

a tired mind
full of wishful thinking,
and a tired smile
buoyed by broken promises,

I'm trying
I'm just tired.

LETTER TO MY DOCTOR

How many ways can I describe
being Tired.

It's easy to go with the classics.
Sleepy is a particular favourite,
Exhausted is a hit at parties,
hanging out with the rest of the merry band
Droopy, Drowsy, Weary and Wasted.
Then there's Tired's cousin Fatigued
fancier than Haggard, not as pretentious
as Enervate, or Prostrated,
and no-where near as fun to say
as Worn to a Frazzle.

What can I say
to make you see,
my lines are Flagging,
the beat is Lagging,
it's Played Out and I'm
Tuckered Out,
already Drained the bank,
Spent every penny,
Overtaxed the nickle and the dime,
Sapped of energy,
Empty of originality,
completely Pooped.

What does it matter,
I'm Done For,
Done In,
Run-Down
and Ready to Drop,
this is a new Low,
to have Shattered

the record, Worn Out
till it Petered Out...

Aren't we all
Dog-Tired?
Dead on Our Feet?
Wishing we'd just
Broken Down
so we didn't have
to Burn Out?
I'm Fed Up.

The truth is,
I say the word so often
it's lost much of its meaning.

I have too.

Because
honestly doc,
I'm just so damn Tired.

MY HAND SHAKES

I want to write. I need to write. My hand shakes. Screens burn my eyes. My headaches pound their own beat. My hand shakes. I need help. You need letters and doctors' notes and X-rays. My hand shakes. I wave my hand. Like you'll understand. It hurts. It aches. In the cold. In the rain. When I clutch a pen. When I type. When I hold it wrong for too long. My hand shakes. There's scars. They don't tell the story. Not the pain or the aching or the shaking or how frustrating it all is. How hard it is to write. My hand shakes. I want to write. With my own hand. Lost too soon, too late. Children bounce back. I didn't bounce back. I bounced through hospital waiting rooms. I bounced through X-rays and MRIs and doctors and surgeries and casts and waiting waiting waiting. It's permanent. You ask me questions I don't have new answers for. When will it get better? Why do you ask that? Do you know something I don't? It's permanent. Scribbles turn into scrawls, indecipherable. My hand shakes. You need proof I'm struggling. There's scars and shakes and X-rays that bounced through me and doctors' notes that speak with authority when I have none. My hand shakes. You don't understand when I bear it with a smile. Because I have to. It's permanent. It'll only get worse. No before, not anymore. I've forgotten before, during was a blur. After is permanent. I want to write. My hand shakes. I write anyway. What else do I have? I need to rest. I can't rest. What am I waiting for? I don't have the answers you want. Nothing is permanent. Things can only get worse. It's not my fault. There's no before. Only this.

My hand shakes.

EXCUSES, EXCUSES

They have a lot to say,
> *there's so much left to say.*

We've heard them all before
> *but does that make the sentence wrong?*

They're a liar's refuge,
> *if you choose who to call a liar.*

A poor man's currency,
> *an honest man's tax.*

Deflect from the problem.
> *I'm telling you the problem.*

Reject the solution.
> *It's been marked irredeemably, irreversibly, unre-solvable.*

Hide from your mistakes.
> *Hide from what you can't accept.*

Where does that get you?
> *What is the truth you want to hear?*

Excuses, excuses.
They so often find a way
to justify,
> *to plead,*

to redirect,
> *to realize,*

to obfuscate,
> *to drop the pretence.*

Procrastinate for
procrastination's sake.
> *Speaking out*
> *for all our sakes.*

Where will that land you?
> *You said I could tell you anything.*

Excuses,
what a joke,
>*it's not a joke,*
your sheep's coat
>*I'm not a joke,*
is wearing thin,
>*I'm wearing thin,*
thin as the lies you spin,
>*on these lies we have spun.*

Excuses,
what a laugh,
>*what a mess we've made,*
I fail to see what you gain,
>*to keep this false peace,*
by playing me for the fool,
>*you reap what we've sown,*
am I a joke to you,
>*what is there left to laugh about.*

Excuses,
what a shame,
>*was it worth it,*
you know you won't be taken seriously,
>*to keep your head in the clouds,*
until you stop spewing these preposterous
>*—ridiculous, to act so ignorant—*
excuses,

    excuses,

       excuses.

>*What is an excuse, to you,*
>*if not a trick, a con,*
>*on whomsoever is more convincing*
>*at convincing us all,*

we're making excuses now.

Excuse me,
for pointing it out.

I will not be excused,
for speaking out.

Will you ask me, next
who I am making excuses for?
Or will you excuse yourself
before the excuses can be made.

Excuse you,
for not hearing me out.
There's just no excuse for that.

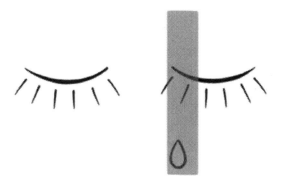

KIDS

I look back on us,
who we were,
and I think—

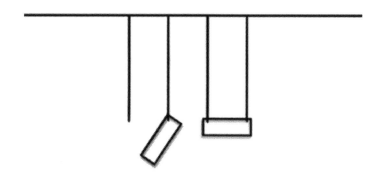

We were really just kids,
weren't we?

PAPERCUTS

It's papercuts
that build and build,
till there's not a page in the house
that isn't bloody around the edges,
and there's not a part of your hands
that isn't covered in bandages.

It's all papercuts,
because you collect papercuts,
easily.

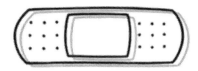

DAYTIME SCRIBBLES

I see a project
completed
before I even put the pen to the page.

Sometimes fear stops me
before I let the ink run
scared the image will fade
with each stroke
decisive
divisive
indifferent to my vision
held to a different standard
one tethered to reality
while my mind wanders in fantasy.

So many ideas
left to disappear
out of a desire
to preserve the ideal.

Some plans fall apart
at the center of a thought

on the crux of a sentence
allowed to lose momentum
dwindle
dissolve
cotton candy too sweet to bear
after those first delicious bites.

What delectable treats
I am the only one privileged enough to taste
savoured on the tip of my tongue
before it sours on its way down my throat
I am rendered hoarse
and unable to share its sweetness.

I witness each dream
as they begin to bloom
choose which to water
and which to let wilt
but a flower must be tended daily
it is so very hard to maintain
mismanaged
mislaid
so often even the strongest flower can't survive
in the presence of an absent mind.

To call it wasted potential
is to assume that you can see the size
of the forgotten graveyard
the ones that didn't get anywhere at all.

I see each project
before I start them
framed in starlight
but all too often
when I reach for them
I find myself grasping at the stars
reflected in the surface of the water

and I've destroyed the image
effortlessly
with one clumsy swipe of my hand
desperately.

Fractured
fragile
watch me
dreaming up a galaxy
and see nothing
but a vacant smile.

COLLECTING
LOST THINGS

I just flit

       and fly

           and float

        through life

             experiences

      hobbies

            dreams

   with no   destination

        and no idea   of which

             will stick

       if any ever will

              isn't that funny?

   to get

       lost

    so

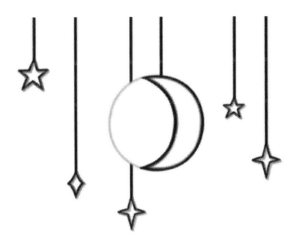

THE MOON

Anyone else look at the moon
for no reason in particular
aside from knowing
that it's there.

BROKEN TREASURES

I am someone who prefers to wait
until the holes in their coat get so big
that I put my head through the pocket by mistake
before I buy a new coat.

I am that vagabond who wishes to see
how many toes can escape my socks
before the sole wears out and I need a new pair
because that's the only way I believe a sock is beyond re-
pair.

It is with an idle precociousness
that I refuse to discard
what should have perhaps
already been discarded.

Instead I will cling to the traces of the past
in the folds of a shirt that no longer fits,
and I will look for the faint marks
that suggests a pen is not yet out of ink.

For what reason, I could not divulge
because I myself do not know what I see
in the damaged things
that I have gathered around me,
lost children who cry silent tears
in shredded stuffing,
real enough, to hold weight enough
that every cracked exterior
adds another scar to my heart.

As a result of these indiscretions
there are items piling up,
broken treasures I refuse to give up,

valuing the pieces that still work
over the parts that just won't.

These irregular artefacts fill my room,
eclipse my space.
A museum or a mausoleum,
it is of no consequence.
Not when I can't begin to imagine
leaving them to rot
in some forgotten garbage heap.

I need it, perhaps
or I convince myself I will,
so that I don't have to accept that I don't.
Out of sight, on my guilty conscious be it.

It's funny, really
how my old coat still holds together.
Must be my conviction and my willpower
to lovingly stitch up each tear
with great care and attention.
For I find myself devoted
to preserving and protecting
old and worn and broken things,
treasures that are no longer treasured,
with perhaps, only one exception—

Me.

A CONFESSION

I lie,
because telling the truth
has never gotten me anywhere
except to pick at a wound
that has never stopped bleeding.

REFLECTING POOL

I sit and I linger and I wallow
in the depths of my thoughts
hoping that someday
I won't feel like I'm

          drowning.

A TENTATIVE
INTRODUCTION

How shall I introduce myself?
No.
That's not right.
That's not the right question.

How do I reintroduce myself?
Which me have you met?
Which me must I fear?
Which me will I wish had been your first?
Is it the me you're looking for
that has caught me in a mess of apologies,
sorry that you had to meet the me
that I can no longer stand to be.

The thing is, there has been many versions of me,
each one beginning shiny and new.
Wide eyes, big dreams
blinking, childlike, into the sunlight,
but like a child who knows no better
I stare for too long,
till those tired eyes start to blur,
and happily welcome the dark again.

Each version of me is a little more worn,
more cracks in the foundations.
There's ivy creeping up the walls,
and another ghost to haunt the attic.
Nothing is more fragile than the mind
when it's had to rebuild a thousand times.

I like to pretend I am reborn,
each and every time,

and that when I begin again,
after I buried my dead,
I will stand with the graveyard at my back.
Yet even now, I place flowers
on the tombs of those that came before.
As if pulling the weeds and helping the lilies bloom
will hide the empty feeling I get staring
at the rows upon rows of cold granite headstones.

There truly is no rest for the wickedness of me.
Not when I seem unable,
unwilling to learn from my mistakes,
the errors that laid my forebears to rest.
Is it not true, that to grow to fit a bigger pot,
you must begin by cutting off the dead roots?

Am I stronger than I was.
I think of this often.
It burns my eyes at night,
staring at the ceiling and
searching for a truth
that no me before
has yet to fathom.

I'm still alive, am I not?

Forgive me,
I have not yet introduced myself,
I fear the power it will grant you
to know this version of me,
not yet buried, and still too new
to know if this is it,
if this is me.

I am me,
I think.

But I can never be sure,
if the me you meet today
will be the me I'll be tomorrow.

ON THIS DAY, X YEARS AGO

Is there a space for me,
carved out

in a fond memory
recalled on a strange night,
my antics bringing out a smile
even after all this time,

in a picture frame
pushed to the back of the shelf,
a reminder of a good story
preserved behind the glass,

in an inside joke
muttered under a hushed breath,
shrugged off in the resulting confusion,
don't worry, you wouldn't get it.

Can I be found
in a familiar look
a borrowed book
an old song
or a funny laugh,
something that is nice,
comforting,
pulled out like an old blanket on cold nights,
when the world's feeling just a bit too loud.

It's funny.
I haven't always intended
to carve out a space.

Some were fleeting, lives I passed through

not stopping for proper introductions.
What name will you call me by?

Others felt like forever, long enough to break
fragile edges to sharper images.
What name do you call me now?

We can't always choose whose worlds we fall into.
We can only hope to leave behind a memory or two
that make us all feel less alone.

I still smile, even if it's strange,
laugh a while, looking back at us,
at the inside jokes, outgrown,
and the photographs, overdeveloped,
we were so young.

There's a space, carved out
inside of me,
the best parts of our best pasts,
taken out on a stormy night
or an rainy morning,
when the world is louder than we are now,
not like we used to be,
overgrown, underdeveloped,
roughly carving out
a space for you and me.

MISSING PIECE

why can't I feel what you feel

why can't I enjoy
the warm heat of the sun on my back
the soothing chill of a cool breeze along my arms

why can't I marvel
at the bright lights of a city as we drive
70 miles along the motorway
or at the peaceful murmurs of nature
when it's just the world and me

what is it I'm missing
the moments of quiet
the daring leaps into the unknown
finding rest while your heart still beats
a cantankerous rhythm against your chest
life, existing

I stand in the rain
I feel wet
stuck to my skin

I curl up in blankets
it's too hot
my mouth is heavy
with the heaviness of a hot chocolate

tell me who has the time
to look out the window
without that lingering sense
of being the haunter
and the haunted

life, existing
but there's too much going on
to simply exist

sitting is uncomfortable
standing is worse
sleeping is a joke
less like a gentle pull
more like a traffic jam

am I the odd one out
strings pulled too taught
to play a gentle note
my feet tap a restless melody

I look up at the night sky
slowly, surely
I become aware of the crick in my neck
the strain in the soles of my feet
the rustling hedges
the bitter pinch of the wind
it's beautiful, the night sky, the moon
I just can't feel it
why is that
what am I missing

how do you wake up slowly
relax with a morning brew
click into work mode
until half past noon
eat, and enjoy the break
find your groove again
discover joy in the little things
the moments between moments

how do you slow down in the rush
of breathing, beating, growing, existing
to look at a flower
and not wonder how it blooms

THE SHALLOW END

I wonder what it's like
to have a pool with a shallow end.

Somewhere to dip your feet in,
ankle high,
enough to float,
as the sunlight warms the water
and the water cools the air,
the ground always inches away.

I wonder what it's like
to be free, to swim
into the deep end,
where the depths are higher
than your hands and your shoulders
and your head,
where you can submerge yourself,
let the currents drag at your legs,
build your strokes,
glide through the water, swim
in the deep end.

You can do that,
because when you get tired
treading water,
you can go back
to that shallow end,
solid ground,
water lapping at your ankles,
so peaceful,
easy, to float
in the shallows.

The deep end will still be there,

once you've had a chance to rest.

My pool doesn't have that.
It's deep all the way round.
Deeper than my arms and my neck
and my head.
There's no place to rest.
Not even as treading water
saps the strength from my limbs,
drags at my heels, pulls
at my ankles and my legs.

It is possible
to get out completely
escape the depths
sit on the edge
stare at a reflection
that almost looks like you
doesn't quite look at you right
blurry from the ripples
distorted in the light
distant
a mirror refracted
by its broken pieces.

The deep end will be there, always
but I wonder if I really want it there at all.

Taking the risk to dive back in,
it gets harder every time.
The water is colder, freezing
the shock of re-entry
snatches the strength from my limbs.
I'm dragging in the currents,
lagging in my strokes,
treading honey not water,
my legs, my shoulders, submerged,

treading concrete,
my head barely breaking the surface.
Take a breath.

What is it like?
To have a pool with a shallow end?
I wonder, and I wish I didn't have to wonder.
Take a breath.

It's all or nothing
in the deep end.
Sinking is much easier
than swimming.
Take a breath.
It's all or nothing.
Will I retreat?
Or would it be simpler
to simply
drown.

BEHIND THE GLASS

She laughed
though, like everything else—

every kind word
every gentle smile
every silly punchline
every cheery anecdote
every soft encouragement
every firm promise
every bright dream

—it was a little fragile.

LITTLE THINGS

There is too much time wasted
in an epic love story.
Wouldn't it be simpler to have one
that was just so-so?

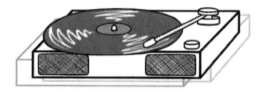

A BROKEN RECORD

Is it love?

To know
and still wish to know,
and take the time to really truly know

To dance in the rain
and wait for the sun to dry your clothes

To seek you out, on purpose

To paint in colour
and make sure to shade in the details

To stand at the point where the rain ends

Is it love?

To see
and still wish to see,
and take the time to really truly see,
the universes between the stars.

LIFEBOATS

We'll find each other someday,
at the right time,
when you don't fear being known,
and I will find the words to tell you
about fears of my own.

You made me brave,
but I have yet to find my voice.
I drew out your smile,
but your laugh still breaks in the middle
like you're startled by the unfamiliar sound.

It's okay.

The best parts of us are still there
and someday they'll show,
and we'll laugh at ourselves
and I'll tell you that I know.

You and me,
we were lost at sea,
but we didn't drown,
not for you,
not for me.

We drifted awhile,
drifted apart, in the end,
on separate lifeboats,
to opposite shores.

It's distance, so often
that forces us to accept
the truth we were hiding
behind warm bodies
and gentle touches.
The truths that we wish
weren't true at all.

That to save ourselves,
we had to learn who we are to ourselves,
to the people we are becoming.
To save ourselves,
when we are not trying so hard to be someone else,
the person the other needed us to be.

To save ourselves,
we had to be selfish.

It's okay.

Someday we'll see
it just wasn't meant to be,
not then,
not for us,
but, someday

Someday, we shall see...

FOREVER WITH A FULL STOP

Forever is a pathetic fallacy,
the rain on the window pane,
the reflection in the rear view mirror,
it stretches on elastic,
forward for eternity,
until it snaps.

Love is not a fantasy
yet, it is imperfect.
It changes
and it grows
and it mellows,
like a song played on repeat,
when the notes stay the same
but the feeling rides on a wave
in a sea that ebbs and flows.

Love is a free spirit.
It takes unexpected roads
and meets interesting people,
follows the birds flying south,
chases the water round the river bend,
and lets the balloon go on a gust of wind.
It can burn as bright as the sun
and it can fade like an old photograph.
But it exists and it existed and it will exist,
even if it doesn't last
forever.

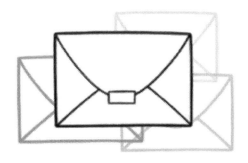

CLOSE TO HER HEART

She has a secret,
you can hear it

whispered in the songs she plays on repeat
the ones that crop up in every playlist
lyrics that make her pause
rewind and replay and restart
they have written the words to her story
in lines sung on a mournful melody
they'll sing it to you too
if you choose to listen closer.

She has a secret,
you can see it

told in the artwork taped to her walls
the prints weathered at the edges
from being carried from home to home
they shared a story with her
in the paper and the ink and the paint
they'll tell you one too
if you choose to peer closer.

She has a secret,
you can search for it

    it's held in the books with cracked spines
    where the corners are a little ripped
    and the pages have to be turned delicately
    thinned from fingers tracing her favourite lines

    it's in the films that she watches on a bad day
    the television shows that skip in the middle
    that one episode that doesn't work right anymore
    worn from multiple replays scratching the silver disc

    it's sitting amongst the stuffed animals on her bed
    those toys she can't bring herself to let go of
    the collectibles still displayed on her shelf
    because who says children must grow out of their
    youth.

She has a secret,
it's not one that can be said aloud.
It's a secret you can only learn
if you take the time to look for it
among the things she holds close.

THROUGH
ANOTHER'S EYES

I write about a love
I don't yet know, intimately
but one that I can see
from afar, all too clearly.

It's broken,
into parts I desire
and parts I detest,
yet glued together
to create art,
the complexity
and the beauty
and the fragility
of stained glass.

Tangled together, irresponsibly
the thorns are a part of the rose, irrevocably.

I find the words to describe a love
that I myself have escaped, so far
but of which can be found in spades
in the places we visit,
and the people we meet,
and the images we develop, oversaturated
enough to wonder if it's really worth it
to understand love at all.

Yet, here I am
writing it all down.
Twisted and sentimental.
Golden and tarnished.
A dream

and a damned thing.

The words of a poet
of love, with a question mark.

THE FELINE INTERLUDE

Be like a cat.
Rest when you need to rest.
Eat when you want to eat.
Sure, you should drink water
but when there's milk left in the bowl
who are you to say no?
Go for a wander in the garden...

or don't.

Find a seat on the best chair in the house,
the throne of judgment,
the prime spot for naps
and some nice, deep stretching.
Steal it if you have to.
Oh, this was your chair?
Not anymore.
Don't apologise,
stare down your opponent,
level them with your best,
then look away first.
They're not worth your time.
You know your worth.

It's time for another nap.

Honestly, be like a cat.
Cats know how to play the game.
They've tricked the whole world
into putting them onto every time-stamp of history,
pictures in every museum and temple,
onto every camera roll and internet app,
because even when cats glare,
or steal your favourite chair,

or knock over that nice glass vase,
it's not their fault.
They're just so criminally cute.

Be like a cat,
take a nap,
catch some sun,
scare some pigeons
later, maybe...

That pillow isn't going to knead itself
after all.

Indulge in a long stretch,
a wide yawn,
take a lap of the room,
find a new nap position,
and be sure to keep an ear out
for that distinct clicking,
a keyboard clacking,
someone trying to work,
so you can be sure to stand in the way
and press a paw,
delicately,
on the backspace.

What's some lost work, to a cat?
They should be paying attention to you anyway.

HAPPINESS

is not the absence of pain
or sorrow or rage or a broken heart.
It's getting so caught up in being happy
that you can forget for a while.

AUTUMN DAYS

I love autumn,
I colour my hair to match,
I shape my person
around a season,
one that's warm
in oranges, reds and yellows,
but is cold enough
for me to cover up,
hide myself in well-worn jackets
and oversized jumpers,
so that I don't have to try.

I love autumn,
a season for caramel lattes,
for scary movies,
spooks and ghoulies.
There's monsters under the bed
to chase away the monsters in my head.
For where else
can you find nightmares that giggle
with childish glee
and candied grins,
but in autumn?

I love autumn,
but autumn, I'm sorry.
A picture can tell a thousand lies.
Flame red hair,
golden leaves,
bright features.
Split ends,
dying trees,
dulled senses.

I love autumn,
I can smile for pictures
with flames in my hair
and a well-worn jacket,
freeze autumn in a single moment,
hold its warmth in that captured shot,
a photograph that speaks of happier times
to carry with me
into the winter months.
For some seasons cast long shadows,
I know all too well.
The frost is not far off,
and soon I will need autumn's warmth
to fight the bitter chill of the long nights
that seek to cut my smile to shreds.

FLYING SOUTH

I think we are all a little like birds.
When people see us flying by
they wonder where we're going,
and they will say South
because that's what they've been told.

SELF-LOVE

They say,
you should learn to love yourself, first.

You're the only person you will live with, always,
isn't that what they say.

I find that hard.

See, I've lived with myself my whole life.
It's been a journey, that's for sure
and I've been along for the ride, at all times,
even when bailing out seemed tempting.

Together,
we've drank and smoked and kissed strangers,
gotten lost in unfamiliar streets,
thrown up, passed out,
lost a shoe, found a penny on the pavement,
what good luck that is!
It hasn't always gone in our favour, that's true.
It's funny, how confident we can get
with a bottle of vodka in one hand and, with it,
an over-inflated sense of our own self-importance.
I handed myself a new drink, regardless.

Together, we've seen a lot, seen enough
I'd hazard, to know there's a limit
to everything, a good time to stop, usually
even if I don't know the trick yet
to getting myself to stop.

I've made all my mistakes myself,
found passions, discarded them, rekindled them,
discovered they could come in different forms.
Cried so hard it felt like my head would explode,

in the dark, where only I would know.
Laughed, do you remember that?
Even when I forgot the punchline,
when I was the punchline,
who decides the punchline?
I forget when it stopped being funny, anymore.

Together, we've seen the lowest I could get,
more than once, learned what climbing up
from the bottom really means,
how it doesn't always work out
the way you want, a shame.
Even when the road seems straight,
there's hidden dips,
turning a corner doesn't mean knowing
what will be there on the other side,
when there's no map or signs to follow,
but it does mean losing sight
of the path you'd just driven.
I'm the only one who has seen
how often I have failed.

So, we've been through a lot
me, myself and I.
Together, we've made our way,
two steps forward, three steps back.
Walking miles upon miles in my shoes
until I had worn my shoes thin.
It's been a ride, that's a certainty.

Truthfully, if I'm being honest with myself
I don't know what it means to love myself,
but I do know I only have myself to blame
because I wouldn't be here without me,
sitting by my side,
the driver in the passenger seat,

fiddling with the radio stations,
offering me questionable directions,
one foot on an invisible brake
and a hand clutching the door release,
pointedly.

I hate me, for that.
I hate me, for a lot.
I look at me and feel pity
for the years we couldn't save, anger
for the moments we chucked away, sorrow
for the person we could have been.

But, it is true what they say
I have lived with me, my whole life
and I am the only person I will know my whole life.
So I know, deep down,
I do love me.
Even though I'd much rather get behind the wheel
of a car driven by someone else.

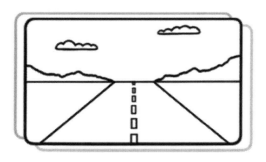

PERCEPTION

Perception is everything.
What curves can be straightened
when looked at from a different angle.
What is left becomes right
in the space of a few steps.
Then there is the one who stands tall,
feet firmly resting on the ground,
who can suddenly find themselves afloat,
unbalanced and upside down,
when the picture is turned around.

FAKER

I like to live in fantasy because
honestly,
real life has failed me and I,
it.

A THOUSAND AND ONE LIVES

I have lived a thousand lives in my head.
A thousand lives where I have been strong,
I have been weak, I have been hurt,
I have fought the odds, and I have won.
In each and every one, I have overcome obstacles
and people and my own fatal flaws.

In these thousand lives I have lived, I have control.
I write and I act and I live in these stories
that I have created and produced and directed.
I choose how they end, how new ones begin.
In each and every one, I survive in a world
I fabricated by my own design.

I am the master in my universe,
I am the puppet and the puppeteer,
and I will decide what's next for me here.

At least, that's what I thought.

But like every story,
over time, the veil lifts
and they no longer shine quite right.
They take on a new glint
one more plastic, packaged and perfect.
Too perfect.
It's easier to spot the flaws
when the image is trying its best to be flawless.

Isn't that a trick?

Because you see,
in all my thousands of lives,

I have written myself against the grain,
created worlds with mistakes in their code,
stepped into personalities increasingly splintered,
to give substance to these lives I saw as lacking.

Isn't it true that there's so much more sweetness
in a character who's suffered and struggled,
knowing in the end they persisted and persevered,
stared down their fate, wearing the face of destruction,
and won in a battle against the threat
of total and complete annihilation.

It's all well and good to be that person
in a story I control,
when even bruised and beaten down I know,
it will all work out in the end, because to that end,
I am the master of my own universe.

At least, that's what I had tricked myself into thinking.

But the truth is, over time,
awareness wears on the picture quality,
knowledge leaves the script lacking,
reality unravels the film reel,
and the narrative falls apart.

It's all in the editing.

The truth is, like every story
I know it's not real, not really.
The world around me, it's not black and white.
It's all colour.

The lives I've lived in my head,
they're nothing more than a fantasy.
An escape from a reality
that suffocates in all its vibrancy.

It seems I'm missing a primary or two.

You can't fix real life in the edit.

So I have found, over time,
I am no longer looking to be the hero, or the villain,
the damsel in distress or the faithful sidekick.

No.

As each life passed by,
fleeting in the grand scheme of things,
rising and falling with the sun,
never longer than a lunar cycle,
I lost my faith in fairy tales
and my love of heroes
and my trust in happy endings.

But I have spent too long dallying there,
in the stories where the villains lose, every time,
and the good guys win,
for how could it be any other way?

I am no longer hoping for a saviour,
but I'm not sure how to be my own salvation.

The truth is, I don't know
what this can mean for me, in the real world,
when I don't always get to write
the lines of my own story,
where every ad lib and unscripted scene
has consequences I can't control, or know,
or trust will work out in the end.

There's no escape hatch, no deus ex machina,
nobody does as expected,
there's no way to predict tomorrow,
there's no ending,

because life doesn't fade to black
once we've found our happiness.

If this was a story, we'd be at the crisis point,
right before the climax.
But this isn't a story, so instead,
it's just a crisis.

Perhaps it would have been fine,
if I hadn't got so swept up
in the worlds I had created,
where dreams come true,
and we confront our own flaws,
grow into better people.

These thousand lives,
that made it easier to survive
outside, where the meaning is harder to find.

It's a truth I not sure yet
if I have the strength to face,
but still, I can't help but wonder...

If living out these other lives
all carefully crafted inside my own mind
hadn't become an escape, an addiction,
a place to retreat when things got tough,
I wonder whether I'd feel more confident,
be more sure of my place,
in this life that I did not choose to live,
but the one that I must live, regardless.

Truth is, I am not the master of this universe, and we are not all stories in the end.

HAUNTER, HAUNTED

I see ghosts,

  in the curved corner of the bathroom mirror,
  in the reflection on the kettle's chrome finish,
  in the frosted glass of the front door.
I see ghosts in the distorted shape of my spoon,
in the corner of my eye as I walk up the stairs,
staring at me with faded features, a vacant expression
when I'm watching the world beyond my window.
There's several, or maybe just one, refracted
in the sharp glint of the knives on the rack,
while another lurks in the darkened oven door.
There's a ghost lingering in my laptop screen,
another dances on the surface of my coffee cup.
I had to put away the mirror sat on my desk,
so I wouldn't get distracted by the ghost trapped there
too.
There's so many ghosts,
the house is crowded with them
littered with them,
  but I can't tidy them away like litter.
I have to learn to live with the ghosts,
walk around with my eyes lowered,
turn off the lights when I enter a room,
as they too have to learn to live with me,
 because ever when I get into bed
hide under the covers, close my eyes

I see ghosts there, too.

MISSTEP

It's hard to feel at peace,
when everything is still unstable,
tenuous,
on tenterhooks,
waiting for a train
you fear you have already missed,
unsure of your step,
but all too sure of the risk,
that comes with relaxing
this close to the edge,
it's a hazard,
there's no safety rail,
and it's so easy
to trip,
to fall again,
become lost in the depths,
of a mind still at work
trying to fix itself.

FOUCAULDIAN

There are many silences.

Thoughtful contemplations.
Tense negotiations.
Peaceful meditations.

The kind of hush that settles after midnight, the witching hour, the refuge of the poets and the artists and the dreamers, and an unspeakable sorrow.

The lull in conversation between friends who have found their rhythm, no need for words to flow steadily to fill the space. It's not uncomfortable, no need to worry. Sometimes it's nice to simply be quiet, together.

The faint hum of the coffee shop, the noise fading gently to the background, indistinct and settling like a burst of inspiration, a thrumming beat under the clacking of keyboards and clicking of pens, as you sit, sipping from a pleasantly warm mug of coffee.

The quiet of the morning, drifting in the tranquil space between sleep and waking, when everything is relaxed and the bed is softer than it has ever been. A somnolent time, before the alarm goes off, chews you up and spits you out, like a used paper straw.

The introspective, retrospective peace of standing at the edge of a forest, at the top of a cliff, close enough to the ocean to feel the spray of salt water, on a snowy path beneath a mountain tall enough it's peaks are hidden by the clouds. When nature speaks, and you listen, voiceless, speechless. Awe, in all its abundance.

The awkward family silences, at the awkward family

gatherings, clammed up with only clammy hand-shakes to offer. When the shaky, uncertain, I-don't-know-who-you-are smiles are met with meaningless platitudes, unnecessary social formalities and a desperate swig from a champagne flute.

The tension when you're sat in no man's land, smart enough to keep quiet, experienced enough to know how to stay small and insignificant, even as the unresolved feelings press pointedly at the back of your throat. It feels loud when you swallow, and every clink of the cutlery, every sip of wine, is louder, slicing through the thick weight of barely restrained anger.

The silence of mourning. Where there are no words, nothing you can say to make the pain go away.

The reticence of nothing meaningful being spoken. When nothing real can be said, because nothing said can be real. When the truth spoken aloud hurts, the tongue a barbed whip that must be held back, even as the silence left untethered cuts deeper.

The moment you take, when you have a moment to take, to think, to feel, in the quiet, dancing in an empty corridor to music only you can hear. A quick double step to the right, a pirouette, take a running leap and land, silently. Feather light. You're flying.

The heavy stillness when the world holds its breath, takes a breath, jagged, sharp, horrified. A ringing silence. The toll of a death bell. *What have we become.*

A moment of silence
please,
for silence itself.

There when we need it,
not always when we want it.
Sometimes an intrusion we didn't ask for,
but so often welcomed in the fall out.
Easy to regret once it's passed us by,
but never leaving without a word spoken.
Treasured.
Despised.
Missed deeply.

Value the silence.
It is too often overlooked, spoken over.
Let it breath.
You'd be surprised how full
a silence can be.

A moment of silence, please
for silence itself.

It give us more than words,
fills voids we cannot fill ourselves,
for when we can't find
the right syllables and synonyms
to capture our thoughts and our feelings
into something with meaning,
the silence will be our translator.

INSPIRATION
INTERRUPTED

Sometimes the words flow like water from the tap.
Other times, it's like trying to open a sealed jar.
You can push and pull and curse and yell
and bang it against the table as much as you like.
It's just not opening right now.

WRITING IN THE DARK

Searching for the words to say
in the light of day

when you can see all the faults
the words stumbled over
the sentences half finished
every crude adjective
and incomplete metaphor

is far more daunting
than closing your eyes
and putting down the thoughts

in messy chicken scrawl
broken syntax and disjointed
line breaks

that plague you at night.

TO BE FORGOTTEN

To be human is to be remembered.
At least that's what I hear, echoing
in the void behind fake smiles,
flat laughs and eyes, empty
of that spark that should make them shine.

It must be hard to admit,
memories are unstable, at best,
as fine as the sand that fills an hourglass,
prone to decay like the old film reels,
and fragile like the paper we print our lives on.

We collect ourselves in artefacts, large in number,
enough to fill a whole museum,
and yet, there's always the risk
that they will all become meaningless,
nothing more than the objects they are,
when looked at through another's eyes.

It's fascinating, watching a world on edge,
trapped by that age old fear
of being forgotten
as fast as you can drop a penny down a well
and hear it hit the water at the bottom.

Hold on.
Cling to the ground.
Grasp at the air.
Plead to an invisible saviour.

How to be remembered?
What is it to be thought of,
when you, yourself, are absent.

Is it as simple as to—

Smile.
Love.
Build a home.
Gather your life in a box of trinkets,
hold an exhibition to a life
frivolously, faithfully, fully lived.

Write.
Sing.
Compose a poem.
Sell your story,
sign your name a thousand times,
hope the ink dries thick and fast,
the paper stays crisp and white.

Scream.
Fight.
Dig your heels into the sand.
Collect letters to your past in glass bottles,
cast them out to sea,
pray that the waves are gentle
and don't swallow them whole.

How do we escape
that uneventful end to our lives,
to be forgotten
in that unremarkable second
that follows your final breath.

I don't have an answer.
And yet, this I know.
One day, near or far,
you will stand before that endless void,
and everything you did
will be standing right there with you.

I hope you're remembered.
I'll try not to forget.

LOST THINGS

Loving, in the moment
is a match, newly lit,
the fire is hot,
hot enough to feel
on the tips of your fingers,
but short lived,
a heat too hot to handle
for longer than the stick can burn.

Loving, in the moment
is discovering a passion as you work,
and delving deeper
with a gleam in your eyes,
to mine that cavern of inspiration,
till you lift your head
and the bright lights blind you,
break your focus,
cut the cord on your line,
let you plummet, backwards,
until you're standing back on the edge of the cliff
unsure how to make that descent again.

Loving, in the moment
is pain, in the aftermath,
as you abandon projects you know
once lit up like fireworks in your mind,
now fizzled to nothing,
a sad sprinkler in a bucket of water.

Loving, in the moment
is living life on the hand of a clock,
losing your balance as the time ticks on
closer to half past the hour,
forced to climb back up at quarter to,

and starting all over again
the next time the clock hits twelve.

Loving, in the moment
is losing it all, in a second.

ALL IN MY HEAD

it's like hiccups.

every time I think,
I've got this—

hic

each time I take a breath,
savour the moment—

hic

when I laugh,
for a second too long—

hic

when I get settled,
into a schedule that seems right—

hic

after a good day—

hic

if I stop—

hic

before I start—

hic

when I make the mistake,
the unmistakable error,
of thinking I have a handle on life—

hic

I hiccup,
and it's like I'm back where I started

but

I have to remember
it's not the same,
not at all

I'm not back where I began
and it's okay to need a break
because a hiccup is not forever—

hic

—and a stumble is not the same as a fall.

UNFINISHED

I can never finish a story

Ideas arrive
Two
     three
         twelve at a time
Crashing over each other in waves
Washing away in the tide just as fast

Words come
Six
     nine
         thirteen at a time
Knocking into each other like dominoes
The picture falling apart on a single misplaced piece

Scenes form
One
     five
         eleven at a time
Passing each other on crossroads
Missing connections on busy intersections

They wait,
unfinished,
crying for closure
and someone to listen to them
and a reader to love them,
as the author moves on—

I love you, but
I'm just not inspired by you anymore.

They're still waiting,
they may wait forever,
I don't know how to find a middle
only beginnings,
and I don't know how to complete anything
only leave them,
unfinished.

WISHFUL THINKING

I cannot forget my past

but

if it could leave me be
just for a moment
I would be grateful to

—*just for a moment*—

forget the expectations
shed the weight
lose the urgency

of trying to outgrow who I was.

CONSEQUENCES

Some things are not meant to be spoken aloud.
Some words are not supposed to be kept locked inside.
Deciding which is which is a choice.

Why?

It has consequences.

STARING AT THE WALLS

This house, it's home.
It has been my whole life.
It's got parts older than me,
that grew up with me,
are a part of me.

There's no place here
in this house
that I haven't wandered.
No nook, no cranny undiscovered.
Though they may say
there is no place like home,
I have found home, wanting.

This house, it's familiar,
mapped out on the soles of my feet.
I know each creaky floorboard,
which windows squeak,
where the carpets bear my imprint,
worn circles paced by tired feet.
I know where every door goes,
where each step will lead,
just like I know every path
will lead me to a dead end.

It beginning to get a little claustrophobic
coming up to a corner and knowing without looking
what will be on the other side.

This house, it always needs some TLC.
I'm struggling against the urge
to paint the ceilings pink,
take a sledgehammer to the walls,
and replace all the light fixtures

with neon bulbs.

Wouldn't that be wacky?

I sit in the same seat,
I walk down the same stairs,
I wake up to the same pockmarked ceiling.
I look out the same window,
and see the same quiet, dead-end street.
I stare at the same reflection
in the same bathroom mirror,
except it's not the same reflection,
it's taller, fills up more of the space,
it isn't as familiar to me
as the blue shower tiles
that I see on the wall behind me.

Can you feel trapped in a house
you are free to leave?

My home, it's not changed much.
I'm fighting against the desire
to throw out all the furniture
and rip up all the carpets,
to see if I can breathe easier
when I'm sitting in my house
when that house is an empty shell.

Would that make me happy?

Truth is, I'm selfish.
This house, it's lovely.
It's home to a lot of good memories.
But it's a place that requires you to move away
to work on your personality.

So I moved away,

I found myself far away,
I didn't find a home
nothing permanent, not yet,
but I did find something,
and though I'm back now—
It's not the same.
I'm not the same.

The walls aren't closing in,
I'm growing too big to fit within them.

This house, it's been here my whole life,
my childhood has a place in the bricks and the mortar,
the worn carpets and the lived-in rooms.
But nostalgia is best left in the past.

It's like looking through an old photo album,
that crinkles when you turn the pages,
brittle, with softened edges,
and if you look at the pictures too long
the world around you starts to look faded.

This house,
it's still home.
But I would hesitate
to call it mine any longer.

CLICHÉD

I'm breathing underwater,
the waves crashing over my head,
sucking the air from my lungs
and the feeling from my limbs.
Under the water,
the world is quiet,
a gentle static in the ears,
and it keeps me silent
by stealing the sound from my lips.

My heart beats fast like a drum,
there's a marching band stomping,
and stamping,
and stomping again,
across the taught skin.
Drum sticks shake the walls,
as they beat an uneven pattern,
frustratingly failing
to keep a steady rhythm,
and threatening to push my heart
right out of my chest.

I feel lighter than air,
floating in the sky,
trusting my feet to keep me gliding
above the fluffy peaks of the clouds.
I feel lighter than the mist that settles
over the mountains on sleepy mornings,
lighter than the steam that curls
from the top of my coffee cup,
lighter than the air that blows from my lips
to skirt across the surface of the liquid
and cool the drink.

I feel so many things,
it's overwhelming,
like falling into a haystack full of needles,
or letting a bull roam free in my head.
Be gentle now,
don't laugh too loud,
more times than not it does nothing to cure my ails,
because truth be told,
though it glitters, my smile isn't golden,
I cry over every spilt drink,
and nothing feels fair
when you show me affection
after we've exchanged I hate you's.
Time keeps cruelly cutting my stitches.

It's clichéd,
I know.
But then again,
if it's clichéd
then surely it's familiar,
and if I'm full of clichés
as common as flipping a penny
and getting either heads or tails,
I guess I can feel comfort
knowing that means I'm human after all.

BITTER PILLS

Love is as likely to be the knife,
as it can be the stitches.

A TOKEN FAREWELL

I'm sorry

I can't wait.

For you to learn the error of your ways.
For you to get your shit together.
For you to see that this is wrong.

We're walking on eggshells, on hot coals
through minefields, mapping safe paths
to avoid hidden pressure points,
telling lies like they might become truths
if we say them often enough,
picking truths like they're pick and mix.
Which ones can you stomach?

I can't wait

I'm sorry.

Your life is leaving
out the front door
middle of the night
bags packed
door on the latch
so you won't know
it's gone
till it's too late.
It might already be too late.
Can you stomach that?

I'm sorry

but I'm tired.

Of walking on eggshells,

on broken glass,
of having to pretend
my feet aren't bleeding.
Keep the peace
don't make waves
don't do anything.

Sink.

This house is a mirage.
It's full of smoke,
the mirrors are cracked,
the truths are poisoned apples
and the lies burn like liquor,
like cigarette smoke,
like pills swallowed dry.
Don't ask me to stomach this.

I thought I'd built a barrier
between me and you,
made of brick walls and window panes.
A parody of the home we lost.
I fear the windows are fogging over,
glazing over,
beginning to reflect back on us.
I don't want to see the day
when I look through the glass
at you,
and see me staring back.

I'm sorry,
I couldn't stomach that,

and I'm sorry
that I can't wait.

For you to realize what could have been,

what we could have built, if you had been willing
to change,
to make amends,
to say sorry.

You're never going to say you're sorry.

It's seems I've made an error
waiting to get my shit together
because I know this is wrong.

I have to pack my bags
put the door on the latch
leave at night
before my life goes on without me too.

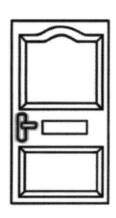

FIGHT OR FLIGHT

You can shatter every mirror in the world,
but you can't escape your own reflection.

TREASURED POSSESSIONS

A pair of socks,
holey,
a toe or two
poking through,
mismatched,
multi-coloured,
wearing out at the sole.
Don't toss them away just yet.
They still fit.
They're not finished.
That pair of socks.

GROWING PAINS

there's growing pains

they ache like a wisdom tooth

do you feel wiser yet?

there's a pop a crick a click

something slotting into place

do you feel taller yet?

there's a tension in your back

burning like a pulled muscle

do you feel stronger yet?

when it cuts

a slicing searing pain

ice in the veins

tingling

skin stitching itself back together

do you feel alive yet?

growing pains ache crack burn bruise

reminders that every step you take

there's nails on the floor

rocks glass nails on the pavement

preparation for every breath you take

there's poison in the air

thick cloying smoke in the atmosphere

do you feel safe yet?

every bone

every muscle

even vein pumping blood

through your beating heart

your expanding lungs

your brain on overdrive

it's all growing pains

to build a person that moves

and a mind that thinks

and a life that lives

in a world that feels real

do you feel grown up yet?

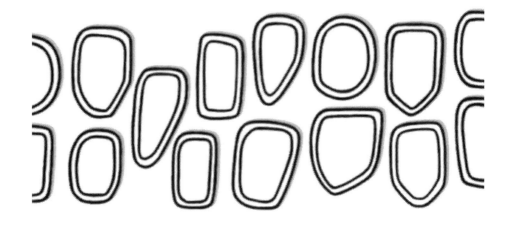

SPEAKING INSANELY

It is madness to think
that madness is what breaks us
or makes us when the truth is
we're all mad here for thinking
that madness is all we have
when we've lost ourselves
in this mad world
of mad dreams
and madder people
running on tanks
full of madness
and aspiration
inspiration
found in the depths
of a mad mind
who dreams up
a mad genius
asking a genius madman
round for tea

and a debate
which descends
quickly and thoroughly
into madness. . .
who can find me that spark of madness
in this maddening state of affairs
who can show me what it means
to be mad in this world run amok
in the fumes of insanity
so that we do not forget
in our mad rampage
who led us here
crying
the pleas
the bargains
the desperation
of the
very
very
very
mad. . .
for we are not alone in our madness
or treated well for our sanity
if to be sane is to speak
in mad voices and loud tones
because above all
we must ask
in our madness
to those who choose
to find us guilty
before innocent [how mad!]
the question we are losing our minds to ask. . .

Aren't we all mad here, sir?

CARDED FOR DRINKS

I still get carded for drinks,
baby faced,
yet I'm barely standing,
body rebelling,
like I'm already on my way out.

I chase the dreams of a child,
fresh faced,
except these days it's harder,
back breaking,
like catching crabs with a butterfly net.

Age isn't wisdom
but it sure feels like it is.

My mind races with ideas,
with the freedom to think,
to think like a student,
to learn and debate
and find flaws in the documents we cherish
and the beliefs we are told to hold true
and the history we put on a pedestal.
The freedom to read
between the thousands of lines
on the faces of men
not carded, elected,
who tell us that they know what we want,
what we need,
why we're dying in jobs that we hate
and on the streets that we walk
and in the homes we can't own,
drowning in debt we can never repay
when school costs too much
and minimum wage is unliveable.

The freedom to say
why we're sick and tired of it all.

I'm older now, old enough
to see the truths, harder to swallow
under the lies, easier to hear
too easy to tell.

Except I'm told
I'm too young to know anything,
like age is wisdom
though it sure as hell doesn't feel like it anymore.
In fact, it's like I'm shouting in a vacuum
while you're firing back in an echo chamber.
Pointless.
I suppose it must be hard to think
when you can't hear yourself speak
over the cycle of bullshit screaming back.
When does it end?

How do I tell you I don't care?
When I do care.
I just don't care what you think,
when you won't care to listen.

Because I'm dying like I'm a hundred
and I'm dreaming like I'm six,
and I'm learning like I'm eighteen,
fresh faced and learning about the world like I'm nine-
teen,
baby faced and learning that the adults have been screw-
ing it up like I'm twenty,
am I screwing it up now?
realising that none of it matters like I'm twenty one,
am I old enough to screw it up now?
I'm still drinking like I'm fifteen,
back breaking, body rebelling.

Life is playing me a broken record.
I'm too young, too loud to be heard,
grow up, wise up,
children should be seen not heard,
be more mature, act your age,
listen to your parents,
they struggled for that life
you haven't earned
and that education
that doesn't mean anything.
You've failed,
to live up to those expectations,
those dreams and aspirations,
because you still don't know anything.
I guess school doesn't teach you anything.
You're an adult now, quiet now,
the adults are talking.
You're too young to understand.

So I'm carded for drinks.
Doctors are telling me I'm too young,
too healthy to be sick.
Adults are telling me I'm too young,
too stupid to be smart.
I'll learn what the real world is,
when I'm older.

But I am older.
I can vote,
I can drive,
I can die in some foreign war,
or on the slip road,
or in my sleep.

I'm old enough
that you remind me

that I'm old enough
to do this, that, everything
but speak my mind
listen to others
form my own opinions
make my own decisions,
take action,
actions that don't revolve around
keeping the status quo
the one that screws you, me, everyone.
I can't remind you of the choices
taken out of your hands
by force, by government, by bigotry—

Times have changed...
Back in my day...
You're not old enough to understand...

Stop.

I am older now,
and I'm always getting older,
and I won't stop,
I'm still learning,
and I'm learning so much.

Age isn't wisdom, no.
Age is easy, it's every day.
A step you don't need to think to take.
A breath you don't need to think to make.
Wisdom is hard, it's the choices you make.
The ones you don't.
It's a fight, it's taking a stand.
It's starting a fire to put out the bigger one
that's been simmering beneath us for years.
The frying pan was never safer than the flames.

It's jagged, and it's barbed,
and it's starting to drain—

My mind.
My health.
My heart.

Don't stop, can't stop, age isn't wisdom, you don't grow up in stages, you won't fit in their boxes, remember, a word spoken has consequences, a silence held has consequences, you know more than they say, don't stop learning, reading, speaking, thinking, you can't trust the adults to save you.

Perhaps that's what they mean by
I'll understand when I'm older.
What they mean to say is
you'll understand when the world's finished breaking you.

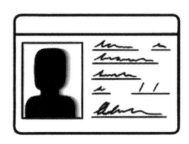

CONSCIOUS ACTIONS

We can never know what the future holds.
We can only keep working to make sure
it's still there when we get to it.

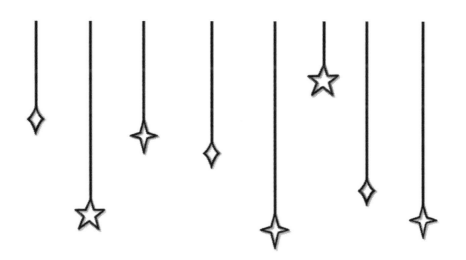

STARGAZING

I think it can be harder to see
what can be
when the sun is shining
on what already is.

The night can be full.
Possibilities, as plentiful
as the stars in the sky.

Think,
each one is a choice, a future,
a place to explore.
They shine bright,
even from afar.
Look to that furthest point
out there, in the inky black,
and see the path winding
from shining star
to shining star.

Believe,
the moon doesn't burn.
Unlike the sun
it doesn't blind,
not like we are blind
to the beating of our hearts,
the rise and fall of our chest,
in the daytime
when we see only ghosts,
ghouls, the weight of their gaze
expecting and unrelenting,
unrepentant in the daylight.

Trust,
this isn't all there can be.
Not when the sun still sets,
the moon still waxes and wanes,
as the sea breaths,
    in
        out
           in
               out...

Please,
take a beat.
Don't escape into your dreams so quick.
Breath.
    In
        Out
           In
               Out...

Sure,
it may all seem bleak,
watching the sky burn to black.
But consider taking a chance on the night,

the sky is not so empty,
and it might all look better
in the softer light of the moon.

SUNSHINE AND RAINBOWS

She thinks everything can be sunshine and rainbows
if she can just shine brightly enough.
Make art with spilled paint,
dance without a stage,
scribble on the walls
when the paper runs out,
speak fluent gibberish,
mime silly characters,
perform to the bathroom mirror,
to an audience of one.

She knows she is strong to glow so fiercely.
Be the sunshine and the rain,
break apart into a million stars,
and embrace the world in the reflection of her tears,
press smiling lips against frosted windows,
laugh against the growl of a thundercloud,
and call on all of the broken parts of her to sing
so elegantly that the birds join in.

She believes she can be the light she couldn't find
at the end of the tunnel she almost never reached.

Who are we to tell her that she is wrong?

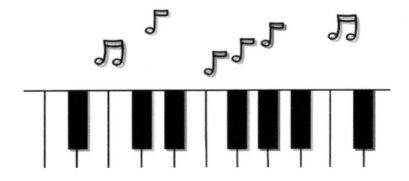

TRAVELLER'S GUIDE

I have found you will wander
through many an interesting and exciting place,
as too, may you stumble,
find yourself tripping,
over many cracks in cobbled pavements
and many roots that break through
on woodland paths.
But, as you pass by each wonderful
and intriguing vista,
remember it as a point on your map
and a stepping stone,
one that, when skipped, sends out ripples.
It is a part of your journey
through dark nights and cloudy skies,
until you find a place you can lay
your own foundations
with which to build something new.
A place that another may walk through
looking for that special place of their own.

THE SHATTERED MIRROR

Do not fret
if you find yourself in the dark.
If you let go of the crumbling edge,
a handhold of roots rotted at their core,
and find yourself alone in the dark.
If you discover there's lights
only when you find yourself falling,
tumbling down the rabbit hole.
If you smile when you hit the bottom,
happy to feel the pain as the impact hits,
elated to finally breathe the air
knocked back into your lungs.
It's okay to sigh in relief
when you drink the poison
that makes you feel two feet tall,
so you can find a door you can open
and a path you can follow.
If this is the first time,
in a long time,
you've seen the world in colour.
If it feels unreal, surreal
at first, second, third look

it's okay to dawdle, explore,
paint the tea set
and smell the roses.
Take your time,
time will wait,
you're on your own time
and time will always tick on.
It's a long way back up,
but do not fret
if you find you are glad you let go.
If you smiled and snickered and sniggered,
giggled and guffawed the whole way down,
and looked to the world like you found it funny
to finally hit the ground.

Even a glass gives a twinkling laugh,
as it shatters.

LETTING GO

often means accepting
that not every wound can heal
without a scar.

ACKNOWLEDGEMENTS

Normally, I am useless at thank you's, but I did force three of my favourite people to read the rough copy of this book before I polished it up, and for them I will do my best.

First, to my father, who has seen more drafts of mine than anyone else. I appreciate every comment you have ever made, even for this book, when I know poetry is not a familiar medium to you. My biggest cheerleader, your support means more than I can say.

And to my friends, who from first hearing of my latest pique of insanity [writing a poetry book, hah!], have made it easier to speak about, by making it something we could laugh about, together. Karla, Calypso, I never thought you'd ask for a limerick, and I was gonna do it, honest. Give it a try. You would have laughed at the attempts, I promise. But I gave up. Never was one for a structure, I'm afraid. I'm gonna have to let you down this time. I know you'd never think I was gonna give you the run around, and in every other way I wouldn't desert you. But this is getting long, and I never said I was gonna write something to make you cry. Never said I was gonna write anything at all really, so I shall say goodbye for now. Best to leave with a promise that I am never again gonna tell a lie and not give you what you asked for. After all, it would only hurt you.

Ah well, guess we'll just have to roll with the punches, eh Rick.

ABOUT THE AUTHOR

Sarah Pledger

This author drinks far too much coffee and dreams of the day where she can afford a house within which she may live with her thirty fur babies. After discovering a love of poetry from a creative writing class at university, learning [for the first time] that not every poem had to be a sonnet, she started a journey that ends at this book.

It began on her phone's note app, where she jotted down whatever spark of an idea came to her, no matter where she was. On the bus, in the bath, while walking - a somewhat dangerous activity that fortunately has yet to result in a collision - and occasionally in more sensible locales, like at a desk. All too often these thoughts gripped her in those moments before sleep, promptly destroying many nights of slumber with the urgent need to get everything down before it could be forgotten. Unfortunately, the author had yet to discover night mode on her phone.

It's seems this is how a poet is born; sleep deprived, heavily caffeinated, and too overwhelmed with an abundance of ideas that she releases them in short bursts of questionable structure and nearly non-existent rhyming pattern. Nonetheless, she is grateful to have finally accomplished her longest and most troublesome goal. A book, of which words have been written and sentences have been constructed. Fabulous.

So Many Thoughts Start With The Letter I

Printed in Great Britain
by Amazon

48977709R00088